Road Trip

Sue Leather

Series Editors:
Rob Waring and Sue Leather
Series Story Consultant: Julian Thomlinson
Story Editor: Julian Thomlinson

NATIONAL
GEOGRAPHIC
LEARNING

CENGAGE
Learning·

Australia • Brazil • Japan • Korea • Mexico • Singapore • Spain • United Kingdom • United States

Page Turners Reading Library
Road Trip
Sue Leather

Publisher: Andrew Robinson

Executive Editor: Sean Bermingham

Editorial Assistant: Dylan Mitchell

Director of Global Marketing:
Ian Martin

Senior Content Project Manager:
Tan Jin Hock

Manufacturing Planner:
Mary Beth Hennebury

Contributor:
Vessela Gasper

Layout Design and Illustrations:
Redbean Design Pte Ltd

Cover Illustration: Eric Foenander

Photo Credits:
40 Pinkcandy/Shutterstock
41 Kpegg/Shutterstock
42 Alexander Biznover/Shutterstock
43 jaume/Shutterstock

ISBN-13: 978-1-4240-4883-0

ISBN-10: 1-4240-4883-4

National Geographic Learning
20 Channel Center Street
Boston, Massachusetts 02210
USA

Cengage Learning is a leading provider of
customized learning solutions with office
locations around the globe, including
Singapore, the United Kingdom, Australia,
Mexico, Brazil, and Japan. Locate your local
office at:
international.cengage.com/region

Visit National Geographic Learning online at
NGL.Cengage.com

Visit our corporate website at
www.cengage.com

Contents

Background Reading

People in the story

Ying Chu
a nineteen-year-old
economics student at
Brenton College

Ash Browning
a nineteen-year-old
business student at
Brenton College

Harrison Morgan
a twenty-year-old law
student at Brenton College

Samorn Sutapa
a nineteen-year-old law
student at Brenton College

The story is set in Brenton, a college town in the
northwestern United States, and on the road from
Brenton to Joshua Tree National Park in California.

3

I don't like road trips

What is that? thinks Ying Chu as Ash drives up in his van. The van is red. It's dirty. *It looks, well, old,* thinks Ying Chu. Are they really going to California in that?

"Hi. Sorry I'm late." Ash puts his head out the window of his camper van and smiles.

Ying Chu is waiting at the door of the girls' dorm. She has three big bags in her hands. "You're always late," she says, but she smiles, too. "It's ten o'clock. Harrison and Samorn are waiting for us."

Ying Chu walks to the van. Then she stops, puts the bags down, and says, "Is this it?"

"What do you mean?"

"Do you really think this can get us to California?" asks Ying Chu.

"Yes, it can," Ash says. "It's great!" He gets out of the van and runs to help Ying Chu. "Wow!" he says. "That's a lot of things for just six days, isn't it?" He opens the back doors and puts the bags in.

"I need all this, Ash," says Ying Chu. "We're going to the desert. Anyway, I have my running things."

Ying Chu likes running. She runs five miles every day.

Ash laughs. "Come on!" he says.

They get in the van, and Ash looks at Ying Chu. "Thanks for coming," he says.

Ying Chu smiles at Ash, but she looks at the van. *It looks really old,* she thinks.

Ash looks at her face. "Don't worry," he says, laughing.

"This is my first road trip," she says. "I usually like to know what I'm doing before I go. I like to go on trips with a plan."

Ying Chu remembers her trip to Boston in October. A small hotel. Breakfast and dinner at the same time every day. Planned trips to see things in the city. Really nice. She's only on this road trip because Ash and the others are her friends.

"Plan? There is a plan," says Ash. "You and me, Harrison and Samorn, a camper van and lots of time to get to the music festival." He smiles a very nice smile. "And The Jaguars!"

"I love The Jaguars," says Ying Chu. "They're great."

"Yes, they are," says Ash. "Come on, let's get the other two."

Harrison and Samorn are waiting at the Cascade Café.

"Here you are!" says Samorn. "I'm cold."

"What year is this van, Ash?" asks Harrison as he gets in. "It's old, isn't it? Are you sure it can get us to California?"

Ash laughs. "Why does everyone say that?" he asks. "This van is OK. Look at it! Look at the kitchen! It's great for a road trip."

Ash starts driving. It's a beautiful day, and in a short time the friends are talking and laughing. As they drive, they start to have a good time.

"Look at this," says Ying Chu, looking out of the window. "It's really green."

"It's very nice to be out of Brenton!" says Ash.

"Yes," the others say.

"No study," says Harrison. "And no classes!"

"We can just have a good time," says Ash.

"California," says Samorn. "Yeah!"

They all laugh at Samorn.

Maybe this will be OK after all, thinks Ying Chu as she looks at her three laughing friends.

Later, Ying Chu opens one of her bags and she takes out her phone. She looks for a road map to Joshua Tree National Park. "Look," she says. "The trip to the park takes 18 hours and 53 minutes. It's 1,265 miles by the really fast road. That means we can drive some hours today, maybe stop here—Grants Pass—then tomorrow night we can be in California. Sacramento, maybe . . ." She shows the map to Harrison.

"Hey, wait a minute," says Ash. "The music festival starts on Friday, June 26. We have three days to get there. We don't need to drive on a really fast road. We can, well, go slowly. You know, go off the fast road—the highway, I mean."

"Go off the highway?" says Ying Chu. "No. I think it's good to get there in time for the music festival. I want to see The Jaguars."

"Yes, Ying Chu's right," says Harrison. "We can look at the National Park before the festival starts. They say the trees there are really different."

"Good idea," says Samorn. She smiles at Harrison.

"Lots of people go to the festival," says Ying Chu. "We need somewhere good to camp."

"That's right," says Harrison. "I really think, Ash . . ."

Harrison, Ying Chu, and Samorn are looking at Ash.

"But we have a lot of time," says Ash.

"No, we don't . . ." start Harrison and Samorn.

"Maybe I can drive?" says Harrison.

Ying Chu puts up her hand. "Wait," she says quietly. "We're tired now. How about this? Let's get to Grants Pass.

It's about six hours from here. We can stop early for the night, have some food, and just have a nice time. Then tomorrow we can talk about the trip. What do you think?"

Chapter 2

On the road

The next day, Ying Chu gets up at 7:30 in the camp next to a river at Grants Pass. There are lots of trees and small tables.

Samorn is sitting at one of the tables. "What a beautiful day!" she says.

"Yes," Ying Chu says. "Sleep well?"

"Great," says Samorn.

Five minutes later, Harrison and Ash come out.

"What about some breakfast?" asks Ash. "We have some eggs and bread."

"OK!" says Ying Chu. "We can eat at the table here."

Ash cooks the eggs. In five minutes, everyone is eating and happy.

"I love camping," says Ash with a big smile on his face.

After breakfast, the four of them sit and talk.

Ying Chu takes out her phone and shows them the map. "It's ten o'clock now," she says. "I think we need to take this road here. That's a good plan."

"Yes," says Harrison. "Let's go . . ."

"OK, OK," says Ash before Harrison can go on. "Let's not start that again. It's my van and I'm driving."

"Well, OK," says Harrison, but he doesn't look very happy.

"But . . ." Ying Chu starts.

"No, Ying Chu," says Ash. "It's OK. Really."

The four of them get in the van and Ash starts driving. They don't speak much for an hour or two as they look out the windows at the beautiful trees and flowers. Then Ash asks, "What do you think of the camper van? It's great, isn't it?"

"The beds are OK," says Ying Chu. "Well, good, really."

"Yes, not bad," says Samorn. "But the bathroom is very small."

"There are bathrooms at the camp," says Ying Chu.

"They aren't very nice," says Samorn.

"I think they're OK," says Ying Chu. "This is camping, Samorn."

"Yes, this is your first time camping," says Ash. "It's usually like this."

"But . . . aagh! What's that?" says Samorn. There's a big noise. It's coming from the van.

"Nothing," says Ash.

"Nothing?" says Harrison. "Stop the van and let's take a look."

Ash stops the van just off the road. He runs to the engine. The others hear noises. A kind of *clunk, clunk.*

Then Ash gets back in the van. "Everything's OK." He smiles a big smile as he starts driving again.

"What is it?" asks Harrison.

"Oh, nothing," says Ash. "Something in the engine. It's OK."

"OK?" Harrison says. He laughs.

Ash doesn't say anything.

They drive on for an hour or two. Ying Chu, Samorn, and Harrison play some games in the back.

As they play, the three friends talk. "I'm worried," says Harrison to Ying Chu and Samorn. "I don't think this van can get us to California."

"Yes," Samorn says, "and where are we driving now?"

"I know what you mean," says Ying Chu. "But maybe it'll be OK. Let's read about Joshua Tree National Park."

Ying Chu takes out a book from her bag. It's a guidebook for Joshua Tree National Park.

"Listen to this, Ash, everyone," she says. She reads from the book. "The Park is very big, 1,250 square miles, and it's in two deserts—the Mojave Desert and the Colorado Desert."

"Wow!" says Harrison. "1,250 square miles!"

"It's famous for the Joshua tree," Ying Chu goes on. "It has lots of desert animals like coyotes. It has rattlesnakes, too. Look at this."

Samorn looks at the pictures of the coyote and the rattlesnake.

"Rattlesnakes?" Samorn says. "They're very dangerous, aren't they?"

"Very dangerous," says Harrison. "Very, very dangerous . . ."

"Don't!" says Samorn. "I don't like snakes."

"It's OK," says Ash. "We just have to watch out, I think. You know, don't walk in rocks. That's where rattlesnakes live."

"The park can get very hot in June," Ying Chu goes on. "You must have lots of water."

"We can get some more water later," says Harrison, "when we get to the park."

Ash drives on. The others talk about the music festival in the back of the van.

Later, Samorn looks out of the window and says, "Where are we? I'm sure this isn't the road to Sacramento."

Ying Chu and Harrison look out of the window.

"No," says Ying Chu. "This is a small road. Look! It says 'Lake Tahoe.'"

"Lake Tahoe?" says Samorn. "Where are we?"

Harrison and Samorn go to sit next to Ash. Harrison looks at the road and looks at the map again. "Ash, we must go onto a fast road," he says. "You're driving to Lake Tahoe. You're on this road here." Harrison tries to show it to Ash on the map.

"It's OK," says Ash. "We have lots of time."

"No, we don't really, Ash," says Harrison. "Why don't you stop driving? I can drive for an hour or two."

Ash looks at Harrison. "Harrison, you're telling me what to do."

"I'm not, really I'm not . . . it's just . . ."

"Just what?" asks Ash.

"I don't know," Harrison says. "I'm just worried that we're in an old camper van that makes noises, and you want to drive all over California."

"I am not driving all over California," says Ash. "And the van is good."

"Mmmm . . ."

"Come on, Ash!" Samorn says. "We just have to get on the right road."

Nobody says anything for a minute or two.

Then Samorn says, "I can drive for an hour . . ."

"That's a good idea," says Harrison. "Samorn is a really good driver."

"No, I don't think . . ." Ash starts.

"But listen, Ash, you're tired," says Harrison. "Why not sleep? Samorn and I can drive and get us back on the road."

Ash doesn't speak, but he stops the van. He gives the keys to Harrison and goes to the back of the van to sleep.

"OK," says Harrison to Samorn and Ying Chu. "Don't worry." He studies the map. "We're really just about eight or nine hours from Joshua Tree National Park." He smiles at Samorn. "You drive for an hour or two. Then I can drive. I feel great. I can drive all night."

Samorn takes the keys of the van and starts driving.

As they start again, Ying Chu looks out the window and thinks about her trip to Boston. In a very short time she is sleeping.

Chapter 3

In the desert

"Aagh! Look!"

Ying Chu hears Samorn's calls. Ying Chu gets up and sees that there's black smoke coming from the van. Harrison is driving.

"It's the radiator," says Samorn.

"It's very hot," says Harrison. He's driving very slowly.

Ying Chu looks at her watch. It's eight o'clock in the morning. What a long sleep! She looks out the window. There's nothing, but desert everywhere. The road looks bad. Nothing for miles, but a few trees. The trees look, well, different. *Joshua trees,* she thinks.

"We're in the park?" she asks.

"Yes," says Harrison. "But I'm not sure where. And I think the van is breaking down. There's a noise and this smoke coming from the engine."

Ying Chu looks at Harrison. He looks very tired. "Just stop," she says to him. "Where's Ash?"

"He's sleeping," says Harrison.

Harrison stops the van. Ying Chu takes out her phone and looks at it. "It isn't working," she says.

"Get up, Ash," calls Ying Chu.

Ash walks up to Harrison. He's very sleepy. He looks out the window. "That's your driving, is it?" he says to Harrison. "Where are we?"

"Me?" Harrison says. "What about this old van?"

"Harrison!" says Ying Chu. "Where are we?"

"I don't know," says Harrison.

"You *don't know!*" Ying Chu says.

"Well, there are three entrances to get into the park," says Harrison.

"Three entrances?" Ying Chu says. "And you have no idea where we are?" Her face is red.

"Wait a minute, Ying Chu!" Harrison's face is red, too. "You get up now and tell me. You're not helping at all."

"It's not me," Ying Chu says. "*You're* the driver."

"Look. We have to drive on," says Ash.

"Drive on?" says Harrison. "But what about the van?"

"It's OK," says Ash. "It does that sometimes."

"OK?" Harrison says. "You think that all that smoke is OK?"

"And now it isn't hot, but in an hour the sun is out," says Samorn. "We're in the desert. It's a hundred degrees in June. And remember the rattlesnakes!"

"And the coyotes!" says Harrison.

"Listen," says Samorn. "I can look at the radiator. I know something about cars. My brother has garages, remember?" Samorn's brother has a lot of garages back in Thailand.

"Well, that's a good idea," says Ying Chu.

"But a hot radiator needs water," says Samorn. "Is there any water?"

Ying Chu looks at Harrison. "Do we have water?"

"Not much . . . I . . . er." Harrison looks away. "Just one bottle."

"You mean there's no water?" Ash says. "Now we really have to go. Let me drive."

Ying Chu is looking at the map in her guidebook. "I think Ash is right. We can't just wait here. We're not really sure where we are. We don't have much water or food, we can't use our phones, and we're in the desert!"

"But what if the van breaks down?" Harrison asks.

"The van is OK," says Ash. "Here, give me the keys!"

Chapter 4

Off the road

"We can't do this, Ash," says Harrison.

"Oh really?" says Ash. "Do you have a different idea?" He is driving slowly down the bad road. He's sleepy.

"Look at the smoke!" Harrison says. Harrison goes to Ash. "Come on, Ash. We have to stop."

"No," says Ash.

Ying Chu watches as Harrison sits next to Ash. Ash is driving, and he tries to push Harrison back. Then the van starts to go off the road.

"Aagh!" Ying Chu calls. "Look out, Ash, there's a tree there!"

But Ash can't do anything. He drives past the tree, but the van goes off the road. It falls over and over.

"Help!"

"Aagh!!"

"What's going on?"

When the van stops, there is a lot of black smoke.

There is no noise for two or three minutes. Ying Chu feels her legs. She is OK. She gets to the door, opens it, and goes out. Ash is on his back on the ground, but he looks OK.

"Where are we?" Ash asks.

"I think we're in an *arroyo*," Ying Chu says.

"A what?" asks Ash.

"It's a river," says Ying Chu. She comes back into the van. "But there's no water in it now because it's June. There are a lot of arroyos in the desert. It's in my guidebook."

"Well," says Ash. "There's no way we can get out of this."

"Aagh!" The two of them hear noises. "Help!" It's Harrison! And Samorn!

"What is it, Harrison?" asks Ying Chu. "Samorn?"

"I think my ankle is broken or something," Harrison says. "It hurts a lot."

They go to look at Harrison. He has his hand on his right leg. His face is white.

Then they see Samorn. She is sitting on the floor. "My hand," she says. "I can't use it and it hurts."

Ying Chu looks at Samorn's hand. "It looks bad," she says.

"What can we do?" asks Ash. "Do we have anything to give them?"

"I have some aspirin," says Ying Chu. She looks for her bag, takes out the aspirins, and gives Harrison and Samorn the aspirins with some of the water they have.

"Well," says Ash. "That's it! There's no music festival for us now." He looks sad.

"Music festival!" says Samorn. She looks at Ash angrily. "You're thinking about the music festival? What about us? We just need to think about how to get to a hospital."

"Well, I . . ." Ash starts.

"And, one more thing," Samorn says. "This is because of your bad driving!"

"Oh?" says Ash. "And what about Harrison driving down this road first?"

"What?!" says Samorn.

Ash, Samorn, and Harrison all start speaking at the same time.

"WAIT!" Ying Chu calls. They look at her.

Then she goes on, quietly, "We are in the desert. We don't know where we are. We don't have much water or food. We can't use our phones. Harrison has a broken ankle, Samorn is hurt too, and in an hour it'll be very hot. We have to do something! Or maybe we won't get out of here . . ."

Chapter 5

A plan

Ash, Samorn, and Harrison don't speak.

"I mean it," Ying Chu goes on. "We need to stop doing this. We all need to help. We need . . ."

". . . a plan?" Ash finishes her words. "But what can we do? We don't know where we are!"

They all think. They look sad.

Then Samorn says, "Let's look at your guidebook, Ying Chu. Maybe we can see where the park entrance is, and where we are."

Ying Chu takes out her book on Joshua Tree National Park. She studies the map again. She looks out the window. "Maybe it's this entrance here, Cottonwood Springs Visitor Center. I'm not sure, but I think we are on Black Eagle Mine Road. Look. It's a small road next to the mountains, just like this one."

She shows the map to Ash.

"It looks like this road starts about six miles from the entrance," she says. "We're maybe ten miles from there now. What do you think?"

"It looks like it." Ash looks at his watch. "It's ten thirty," he says. "If this is it, there are people at the entrance now."

"But ten miles!" says Samorn. "How can we get there?"

"You can't go," says Ying Chu to Samorn. "You and Harrison have to wait here. Ash and I can go."

"But can we really go ten miles?" asks Ash. "It's hot, and do we really know where we are?"

"We *have* to go," says Ying Chu.

"We'll come back in a short time," says Ying Chu as she puts on her running shoes. "With some help."

Samorn looks sad. "We have no water or food and . . ." she says.

"It's OK," says Ying Chu. She smiles at Samorn. "Ash and I can walk ten miles in just over two hours if we walk fast."

"Walk?" says Ash. "We can run!"

"No," says Ying Chu. "We can't run. We don't have much water, and it's getting hot. We have to walk."

"Wait," says Ash. "We'll have to pay to get the van onto the road again."

"Here," says Harrison. He gives Ash some money.

Ying Chu takes the map.

"What about water?" asks Samorn. She puts some of the water into a small bottle. "Here," she says. "You need this."

"This is the only bottle we have," Ying Chu says.

"Take it," says Samorn.

Ying Chu puts it into her bag.

Ying Chu and Ash get back up on the road. They start walking fast back down the road. *Ten miles,* thinks Ying Chu.

The first mile or two are easy. It's hot, but the sun is not too hot in the morning. Ash is walking fast next to Ying Chu. They walk and walk and walk. Two miles, three, four . . . they go on walking.

Ying Chu looks at her watch. Eleven forty-five. The sun is getting hot now. *We're about four miles from the Visitor Center,* she thinks.

After one more mile, Ash stops and sits down. "Aagh," he says.

"What?" asks Ying Chu. She stops, too.

"I can't walk anymore," says Ash. "My legs hurt. I feel bad." His hand is on his head.

Ying Chu takes the small bottle of water and gives it to Ash. "Drink this," she says.

He drinks the last of the water and they wait. "It's no good, Ying Chu," Ash says. "I'm sorry. I can't go on."

Ying Chu waits a moment. "Come on, Ash," she says.

"I can't," says Ash. "I just can't."

Ying Chu looks at the desert. There is nothing. It's very hot now. She looks at Ash and sees that he can't walk. She tries her phone. It doesn't work.

"OK, listen," she says. "You wait here. I'll be back with help."

Ying Chu feels very bad as she starts walking again. She doesn't feel strong. She doesn't want to leave Ash in the desert. She feels very tired now, too. The sun is hot and it's difficult to walk. She walks a mile or two. She sees something in the rocks. It looks like a rattlesnake! She walks away from the rocks quickly. She thinks about Ash. He can't walk—the rattlesnakes! *I have to get to the Visitor Center,* she thinks. *I have to help my friends.*

She walks slowly. Her head hurts. Her feet hurt. Everything hurts, but she walks. Then she thinks, *I can't walk anymore. I have to sit down. No! I can't stop. If I stop, maybe I can't get up.* She walks a short way. Then, she is on the ground. She can't get up. It's very, very hot! Her head hurts. She wants to sleep. She closes her eyes. She opens them again. Then she sees a man. Over there! A man. He's wearing brown pants and a shirt. *This is the Visitor Center,* she thinks. She tries to get to the man. Slowly, she tries to get up. She looks and puts up her hand. Can he see her?

She opens her mouth and calls, "Help!" The man looks at her. Now he starts running to her. She closes her eyes again.

Ying Chu opens her eyes. *Where am I?* She is in a bed in a small room. A hospital?

Two minutes later, the door opens. A man wearing a shirt and brown pants comes in.

The man smiles. "Hey," he says. "You're awake!"

"Wha . . . ?"

"I'm Jack Clark from Cottonwood Visitor Center," says the man. "It's OK. You're OK. You're in the hospital."

"You're a very brave young woman," he goes on. "Your friends are OK because you can read a map and walk ten miles in the desert."

Now Ying Chu remembers the man; she remembers the desert; she remembers her friends. Her friends!

Jack Clark smiles and opens the door again. "And here are your friends."

Then Samorn, Harrison, and Ash come in. They are all smiling.

"You're all OK!" says Ying Chu.

"Yes," says Samorn. "We're all here. Thanks to you!"

"Yeah," says Ash. "Thank you." He smiles at Ying Chu.

"Yes, thanks, Ying Chu," says Harrison. "You . . . well . . . we're here!"

The four friends hug.

"But it's too late for the music festival," says Ash. He looks sad for a minute. "The camper van is at the garage and it can't go anywhere for days."

"It's OK," says Ying Chu. "Really, it is."

"But what about the plan?" asks Ash. "The Jaguars and everything."

Ying Chu looks at her friends and smiles. "I'm just happy to be here, with you," she says.

Review

A. **Match the characters in the story to their descriptions. Use the names in the box.**

Ying Chu	Harrison	Samorn	Ash

1. _____ thinks his van is fine.

2. _____ doesn't like road trips.

3. _____ doesn't like the camp bathrooms.

4. _____ asks Ash to sleep in the back of the van.

5. _____ has a brother who has lots of garages.

6. _____ has a broken ankle.

7. _____ drinks the last of the water.

8. _____ leaves Ash in the desert.

B. **Read each statement and decide whether it is true (T) or false (F).**

1. Ying Chu is worried about the van.   T / F

2. Ash wants to get there quickly.   T / F

3. They stay at a camp on the first night.   T / F

4. A rattlesnake bites Samorn's hand.   T / F

5. Harrison's ankle and Samorn's hand are hurt.   T / F

6. Ying Chu's phone is broken.   T / F

7. Ash goes with Ying Chu to find some help.   T / F

8. Ying Chu runs all the way to the Visitor Center.   T / F

9. They get to the music festival.   T / F

C. Choose the best answer for each question.

1. Ying Chu is going on this trip to _____ .
   a. see Joshua National Tree Park
   b. see The Jaguars
   c. visit some places in California

2. The trip is about _____ miles.
   a. 300
   b. 1,265
   c. 810

3. _____ do NOT live in the park.
   a. Tigers
   b. Rattlesnakes
   c. Coyotes

4. The van falls into _____ .
   a. a lake
   b. the sea
   c. a river bed

5. At the end of the story, Ying Chu wakes up in the _____ .
   a. van
   b. hospital
   c. garage

Answer Key

A:

1. Ash; **2.** Ying Chu; **3.** Samorn; **4.** Harrison; **5.** Samorn; **6.** Harrison; **7.** Ash;
8. Ying Chu

B:

1. T; **2.** F; **3.** T; **4.** F; **5.** T; **6.** F; **7.** T; **8.** F; **9.** F

C:

1. b; **2.** b; **3.** a; **4.** c; **5.** b

Background Reading:

Spotlight on ... *The Mojave Desert*

The Mojave (mo-hah-vee) Desert is in the southeastern part of California in the USA, and is also in Nevada, Utah, and Arizona. It is 124,000 square kilometers (47,877 square miles) and is one of the biggest parks in North America. The word "mojave" is a native American word that means "beside the water."

Not many people live in the Mojave Desert. There are a few small towns—some with only 2,000–3,000 people. The biggest city is Las Vegas in Nevada with 1,900,000 people.

The Mojave Desert has mountains and a few rivers, and many people come to see them. The mountains are full of color. There are many small parks, too.

The Mojave Desert has both winter and summer. The driest and lowest area in the desert is called Death Valley.

In summer, the valley is very, very hot and is the hottest place in North America. It gets up to 54°C! Death Valley gets very little rain and many animals and plants die there.

There is a special tree in the Mojave Desert called a Joshua tree that is famous all over the world.

Think About It

1. Do you want to go to the Mojave Desert?

2. Is there a desert near where you live?

Spotlight on ... *Staying alive in the desert*

Did you know that **33** percent of our land on Earth is desert? Eighty percent of our deserts have rocks and lots of plants, but only **20** percent have sand. Not all deserts are hot.

Many people worry about deserts. They worry there is not enough water or food. But deserts have lots of them. You need to know where to look. Here are some ideas about how to stay alive in the desert.

1. Stay with your car. Do not walk away. People can find you more easily on a road. Try to think people are coming to find you. Do not worry.

2. During the day, don't sit in your hot car. Make something from wood and things on the ground so you can get out of the sun. Put something on your head.

3. Deserts can be cold at night. Find a place to stay warm. Your car will be warm.

4. Start a fire at night. Fire keeps dangerous animals away.

5. Don't drink all your water at first. Drink a little during the day.

6. Find drinking water. Dig a hole in the surface of a river bed. Collect drops of water from plants in the early morning. You can also find water by cutting soft plants.

7. Don't drink water from your car's radiator. Create a solar water still. Put plants (or water from your car's radiator) in a hole. Put a cup in the middle of it. Cover the hole with plastic. Clean water will go in the cup.

8. Put plastic bags over the leaves on a tree. Water will come out.

9. Try not to eat or talk. Eating and talking use water.

10. When hiking in the desert, only travel at night, during sunset, or in the early morning.

Think About It

1. Do you know any more things you can do?

2. What can you do if you are lost in a desert?

Glossary

bottle	(*n.*)	a container for liquid, e.g., water
camp	(*v., n.*)	to live temporarily outdoors, usually for recreation; a place for people to live outdoors temporarily
(camper) van	(*n.*)	a vehicle used for traveling and camping
dangerous	(*adj.*)	not safe; risky
desert	(*n.*)	a very dry area of land with very little rainfall
drive	(*v.*)	to cause and control the movement of a vehicle
engine	(*n.*)	a machine in a car or van that makes it move
entrance	(*n.*)	a place where you go into (enter) a room or area
(music) festival	(*n.*)	a musical performance with a number of singers and bands
garage	(*n.*)	a place where cars are kept or repaired
guidebook	(*n.*)	a book with tourist information about a city or area
hurt	(*adj.*)	feeling pain
map	(*n.*)	a picture that shows the rivers, mountains, streets, etc., in an area
noise	(*n.*)	a sound that someone or something makes
(national) park	(*n.*)	a large area of public land kept in its natural state to protect plants and animals
plan	(*n.*)	a set of actions prepared as a way to do or achieve something

radiator	(*n.*)	a device that is used to keep the engine of a vehicle from getting too hot
rocks	(*n.*)	stones on the surface of the ground
window	(*n.*)	an opening in the wall of a building, the side of a vehicle, etc., for air or light

NOTES

www.ingramcontent.com/pod-product-compliance
Ingram Content Group UK Ltd.
Pitfield, Milton Keynes, MK11 3LW, UK
UKHW020737280225
455688UK00012B/716